# The Story

## of

## YOU

# WORKBOOK

# An Enneagram Guide to Becoming Your True Self

# IAN MORGAN CRON

### and JANA RIESS

HarperOne

*An Imprint of HarperCollinsPublishers*

# The Story

## of

## You

**WORKBOOK**

HarperCollins books may be purchased for educational, business, or sales promotional use. For information, please email the Special Markets Department at SPsales@harpercollins.com.

First HarperOne paperback published 2022

FIRST EDITION

*Designed by Nancy Singer*
*Opener art: @fotokup/stock.adobe.com*

Library of Congress Cataloging-in-Publication Data is available upon request.

ISBN 978-0-06-282578-0

22 23 24 25 26   LSC   10 9 8 7 6 5 4 3 2 1

# CONTENTS

# Introduction: Welcome

I'm so glad you're here!

This workbook is your hands-on companion to my book *The Story of You*, and it's designed to help you get unstuck. The book is about how you can use the Enneagram to figure out what broken story you are telling about yourself. Most of us learned such stories during our childhood and then carried them on into adulthood. But what it meant to be a "good" girl or boy or what made a parent "proud" might become self-defeating in adulthood. The book explains how you can use the Enneagram to uncover these false stories and discover a better one that more accurately says who you are. Allowing more congruence between your true self and how you understand and express yourself leads to more happiness, joy, and freedom. And who doesn't want those?

The Enneagram was never meant to merely identify your personality type;

that's just the beginning. Learning your type is an appetizer. The rich, meaty main course is transformation, and that is what this book and workbook are all about. In the book, we took everyone through the kind of work each of the nine personality types of the Enneagram needs to do, with examples of how real people transformed themselves using the process called SOAR (see below). In the workbook, we will turn this structure inside out, since the goal is to help you go deep into *your* story. So the chapters will be organized around helping you go through the SOAR process of *seeing, owning, awakening,* and *rewriting* your story.

You'll want to take some time with it. My goal throughout is to help you see the ways you're trapped in the grip of your old story—the shadow side of your Enneagram type—and how to get out of it.

*See:* We'll start by doing a deep dive in your past to establish how you came by the story you've been telling yourself about who you are and how you think the world works. Where did that story come from, and why? How has it helped or hurt you?

*Own:* The Own step is all about taking an inventory of both the strengths and the shadow side of your type. Your Enneagram type's story has helped and hurt you throughout your life so far, and it's pivotal to explore the ways that has played out in your relationships, work, and sense of self.

*Awaken:* With this step, our attention shifts from the past to the present. I'll teach you how to "catch yourself" in real time and use the principle of *agere contra* (literally "acting against") to resist the pull of your old, familiar story. It's only when we have the power to stand back and observe our own behaviors that we have a shot at changing them.

*Rewrite:* Now that you've laid the groundwork by analyzing how your old story shaped your life in the past and continues to have a hold on you in the present, you're ready to imagine a new future. This calls for renaming your story and embracing your power to *respond* and not just *react* to circumstances. Taking authorship of a new story is the key to your transformation.

This workbook is something you can do at your own pace. Some people will take a methodical approach and may choose to do one step a week, but that's not necessary. It doesn't matter how long it takes you as long as you keep moving forward on your journey; working through the written exercises; and becoming more mindful of how you are feeling, thinking, and acting. The workbook can be done alone or in the company of others; that's also entirely up to you.

All I ask is that you keep an open mind and be willing to commit your thoughts to paper. The act of writing, as we'll see in the steps ahead, can be a powerful change agent. It will help you understand just how very strong you are.

*Ian*

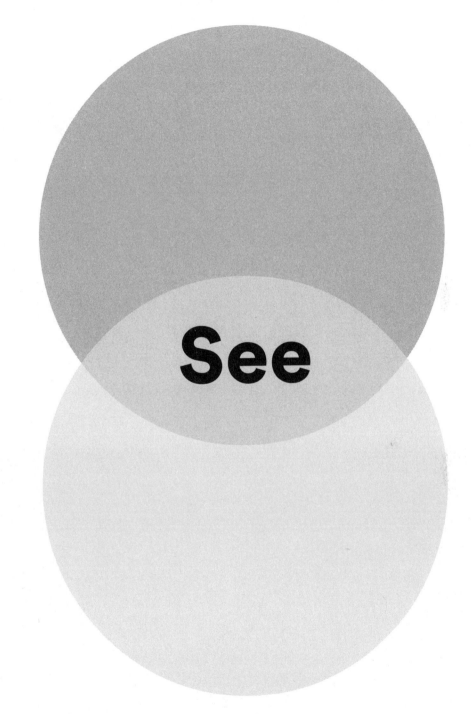
See

# PART 1

# Your Enneagram Type's Origin Story

When you begin recognizing the pull of your type's old story, you can use those moments as opportunities to update the story you're telling yourself and others about who you are and how you think the world works.

*—The Story of You*

We tell ourselves stories in order to live. . . . We interpret what we see, [and] select the most workable of the multiple choices.

*—Joan Didion, The White Album*

The world is a scary place. Most of us spend our childhoods trying to piece together an identity that helps us avoid what causes us pain and experience more of what we all want: love, a sense of security, and some ability to direct our own lives. Our Enneagram personality emerges as part of this quest. It's not our "real" self so much as a familiar tool that helps us navigate the world.

That tool works for us, often well into adulthood, until one day it doesn't. That's when we realize that our personality is actually getting in the way of our true story, obscuring some of the reality of who we are. We've fallen into patterns we don't like and keep unconsciously repeating the same behaviors over and over.

Your Enneagram type is not the full or true story of who you are. However, understanding your type and its mechanisms is an initial step as you begin digging through the layers of buildup that hide that true story. So our first task as we journey toward self-awareness is simply to learn more about the Enneagram and its nine basic ways of navigating the world.

## YOUR ENNEAGRAM TYPE'S STORY

Although we all want the same basic things, people of each type have different ways of obtaining those things, and certain messages they regularly tell themselves about who they need to be to get what they want. Some of those messages are based on mistaken beliefs.

Look at the following table, especially the messages for your Enneagram type. (If you do not know your Enneagram type, you can take a test at *typologyinstitute.com/assessment/*.) Circle or highlight any messages from your type that you recognize you've told yourself in the past. You might not identify with all of them, and feel free to add more to the list. Then take some time to respond to the questions on the next few pages. You may recognize parts of yourself in descriptions from the other types as well. Feel free to circle whatever seems to fit you.

## RECOGNIZE YOUR OLD STORY

| Enneagram | Type No. | Old Story Messages of Each Enneagram Type |
|---|---|---|
| GUT triad | 8 | • When the going gets tough, the tough take charge.<br>• It's not okay to reveal weakness or vulnerability.<br>• It's important to assert strength and control over others and over the environment. |
| | 9 | • The world threatens my inner and outer peace.<br>• To maintain inner harmony, I had better avoid conflict and keep the peace.<br>• It's safer to merge with the agenda of others than to voice my needs, feelings, and preferences. |

| Enneagram | Type No. | Old Story Messages of Each Enneagram Type |
|---|---|---|
| | 1 | • We live in an either-or world. There is no in-between.<br>• I can only be loved if I do everything right.<br>• If I make a big mistake, I'll be blamed and criticized.<br>• There is always more I should be doing to improve myself, others, and the world. |
| HEART triad | 2 | • Other people's needs are higher priorities than my own.<br>• Other people will only take care of me if I take care of them first.<br>• Acknowledging my own needs and asking for help would lead to humiliation and abandonment. |
| | 3 | • The world values people for what they do rather than for who they are inside.<br>• Feelings are messy and time-consuming, and they slow me down from accomplishing my goals.<br>• I have to be successful, look like a winner, and avoid failure at all costs. |
| | 4 | • There's something important, some magic key for happiness that other people seem to have that's missing inside me.<br>• If I'm not special and one of a kind, people won't see me or accept me.<br>• I am my emotions.<br>• No one understands me or how much I suffer. |

| Enneagram | Type No. | Old Story Messages of Each Enneagram Type |
|---|---|---|
| **HEAD triad** | 5 | • Relationships will drain my energy, so I need to be self-sufficient and withdraw from other people.<br>• The best way to protect myself from a frightening world is to be armed with information.<br>• I should wait to act until I have analyzed all the facts.<br>• I have to conserve my time, energy, and resources or I will be overwhelmed. |
| | 6 | • Disaster is just around the corner, so it's vital to be prepared.<br>• I can't always trust my own judgment, so I look to others to guide me about what to do.<br>• I feel safe when I understand my role in the world and contribute to the community.<br>• My anxiety about the future helps me to be ready for anything. |
| | 7 | • Stay on the sunny side, always on the sunny side . . . or I might be overwhelmed by negative thoughts and feelings.<br>• When life threatens to become painful, I need to outrun it by focusing on happy things, new adventures, and the future.<br>• People need me to be "up" for them, but if they can't stop being negative or boring, I should move on. |

What are your earliest memories of how you saw yourself or how others described you when you were young?

Which self-limiting messages from your type ring true about you, and why?

How did the important people in your life ever implicitly or explicitly instill those messages in you? What role did your parents and siblings seem to need you to play in the family?

Think back to when you were in school. How did the "old story" of your Enneagram type get reinforced by your classmates and teachers?

When you were a child, what was your "safe place"? Was there anywhere you could go to be totally and completely yourself?

How did your old story help you make sense of the world?

# NAME YOUR OLD STORY

Several people who are profiled in *The Story of You* gave a name to their old story. For example, Ryan, a Four who never felt he was as worthy of love as the people around him, called his old story "Hand-Me-Down Boy."

**If you had to give a name or a title to your old story so far, what would it be?**

**How has that old story protected you in the past, or helped you gain the things you want? When have you been rewarded for playing that role?**

On the other hand, how has that old story limited your possibilities in the past? How does it continue to do so in the present?

## YOU ARE MORE THAN YOUR ENNEAGRAM TYPE

The good news is that your Enneagram type does not have to define you. Your old story is not who you are. While your core Enneagram number never changes, you can grow into a freer, more evolved version of that core number.

Enneagram experts teach that there are several layers of development within each type, ranging from those who are most "stuck" in their type's default mechanisms to those who are most balanced and free. Look at the following table and highlight or circle where you think you most often fall within your type. We will revisit this chart at the end of the workbook to see if there has been development and transformation.

**Your Enneagram Type's Origin Story**

• • •

| | | | |
|---|---|---|---|
| 8 | Unhealthy | Aggressive, domineering, and intimidating. Has to be the most powerful person in the room. Judges other people they deem to be weak. | Passion: Lust |
| | Healthy | Channels strength and intensity into protecting the vulnerable. Allows self and others to grieve or be weak at times. Listens well and deeply to other people, and apologizes when wrong. | Virtue: Innocence |
| 9 | Unhealthy | Constantly numbing out. Cannot complete tasks. May look compliant on the outside, but angry on the inside. Merges with other people or groups to avoid conflict. Seems "stuck" and waiting for things to happen rather than making things happen. | Passion: Sloth |
| | Healthy | Recognizes own desires and can voice them, even if others don't agree. Can say no and mean it. Invests in their own development and becomes their own person. | Virtue: Right Action |

| | | | |
|---|---|---|---|
| **1** | Unhealthy | Desperate to fix everything and everyone around them. Cannot abide mistakes in others but especially in themselves. Hypercritical and often self-righteous. In the worst cases, secretly acting out the same behaviors they criticize in others. | Passion: Anger |
| | Healthy | Highly ethical, committed, and morally heroic, but also recognizes they don't carry the responsibility to save the world. Can see other points of view and doesn't have to be right all the time. Understands they are inherently good. | Virtue: Serenity |
| **2** | Unhealthy | Manipulates other people's affections through flattery and by "giving to get." Makes self out to be an unappreciated martyr. Does not admit own needs and takes pride in never putting themselves first. Can be clingy and possessive. | Passion: Pride |
| | Healthy | Often chooses to help others, but does not *need* to help others to gain approval. Are generous people, but give of themselves without assumptions of what they "deserve" in return. Humble about the degree to which their help is really necessary to others. | Virtue: Humility |

| | | | |
|---|---|---|---|
| **3** | Unhealthy | Will cut corners or embroider the truth to appear successful. Highly image-conscious and has trouble recognizing their own feelings or those of others. | Passion: Deceit |
| | Healthy | Still motivated and goal-oriented, but also aware that their self-worth is not tied up with a successful outcome. Can thrive without the attention or admiration of others. No longer needs to project an impressive persona. Focused on helping other people succeed rather than only on their own success. | Virtue: Authenticity |
| **4** | Unhealthy | Prone to moodiness, self-loathing, and despair. Unable to maintain equilibrium amid their rapidly shifting, powerful emotions. Needs to feel special and unique. May be looking for a soulmate to "complete" them. | Passion: Envy |
| | Healthy | Compassionate, sensitive, and emotionally balanced. Revels in own creativity and in sharing it with others. Embraces the present and looks forward to the future rather than fixating on the past. | Virtue: Equanimity |

| | | | |
|---|---|---|---|
| **5** | Unhealthy | Aloof, reclusive, and sometimes intellectually arrogant. Cut off from emotions and from other people, and fearful of being overwhelmed by the world. Can become isolated and eccentric. | Passion: Avarice |
| | Healthy | Intellectually alive and curious, but also attuned to emotions (their own and those of other people). Able to enjoy the company of others without fear. Does not overrely on their mental abilities, but appreciates the value of feelings and intuition. | Virtue: Nonattachment |
| **6** | Unhealthy | Excessively fearful and anxious about worst-case scenarios, abandonment, and own inadequacies. May be blindly loyal to a person or a cause. | Passion: Fear |
| | Healthy | Secure in the knowledge that they can make decisions for themselves and handle whatever comes their way. Committed and loyal friends, community advocates, and colleagues. | Virtue: Courage |

| 7 | Unhealthy | Flighty and desperate to be entertained. Cannot absorb pain, so seeks distraction and variety at all costs. Has trouble "settling down" into a job, family, or situation. Prone to impulsivity. | Passion: Gluttony |
|---|---|---|---|
| | Healthy | Channels fun-loving energy into the present moment rather than always looking where "the grass is always greener." Optimistic about the future but no longer needs to escape present realities. No longer overfocuses on the future but can remain in the present. | Virtue: Sobriety |

Where do you recognize yourself in the healthy and unhealthy behaviors in the previous chart? (Most people are a mixture of both.)

What situations or people tend to trigger the unhealthy behaviors in your life?

Think about the name you gave to your old story. How does it describe the healthy or unhealthy parts of your type?

If you could choose just one thing to change about yourself, what would it be?

What would you like to keep?

# PART 2

# The
# Stories
# You're Telling

There's a kind of logic, even genius, to some of the
stories we tell ourselves. Like all myths, though, the story
doesn't capture the entire truth. Our understanding
and perception of certain pieces is limited. And yet
we remain strangely loyal to the broken story we
convinced ourselves as children must be true.

—*The Story of You*

We cannot live the afternoon of life according to the
programme of life's morning; for what was great in
the morning will be little at evening, and what in the
morning was true, will at evening have become a lie.

—Carl Jung

Now that you've given a name to your old story, let's flesh out some details. In this section, you'll be asked to pinpoint the story you've been telling yourself and others over the years, and to determine whether that old story is actually true.

## WRITE YOUR OLD STORY

Set a timer for twenty or thirty minutes. Take these next few pages to write your old story. There's no right or wrong way to do this, so don't feel intimidated. Unless you choose to share it, no one will be reading this but you.

If you need some direction to help you get started, here are a few ideas:

✓ You could write it as a sort of timeline, identifying a few key events in your childhood and adulthood that perpetuated and strengthened your old story. What were five negative events that shaped you (e.g., losses, hurtful words, trauma)? What were five positive events that also shaped you (e.g., achievements, encouragement, your proudest day)?

✓ You could focus on a few pivotal individuals whose influence helped you become who you are today, either because you admired and wanted to please them or because they handed down beliefs that shaped your understanding of who you are.

✓ You could divide your story into chapters, with each chapter a paragraph that's started with a prompt, focusing on how you got *here*, where you are today. Prompts might include: *I knew who I was that day when*... or *The moment when everything changed for me was*...

**Name of old story:**

**Story:**

**The Stories You're Telling**

●  ●  ●

# NOTICE THE PATTERNS OF YOUR STORY

What repeating patterns, themes, ideas, and feelings keep cropping up in your old story?

How did the world or important people push you toward the old story you've been living? How were you rewarded for it?

What does your story reveal about how you see the world? Has your personality developed to become fundamentally suspicious, trusting, needy, overachieving, etc.?

Finally, is the story you've been telling yourself and others about who you are *true*? If not, where does the story fall short of capturing who you really are?

# IMAGINE THE ENDING OF YOUR OLD STORY

Just as you can reclaim power over your life when you recognize and name your old story, you can also find power in imagining how it might end.

So do a little projecting into the future. If the old story continued to dominate your life, what would happen in the following areas as the years go by? In other words, if you never changed any part of your old story, how would that old story play out in the following areas? What would people say about you at your funeral?

**Relationships:**

Work:




Physical health:

Emotional and psychological health:

Spiritual life:

# PART 1

# Facing
# Your Shadow

You don't have to be stuck with your old story, the
default programming that governed the first part of
your life from the shadows but now works against you.
The Enneagram can't transform us unless we're
rigorously honest with ourselves about who we are.

*—The Story of You*

Each Enneagram type has weaknesses and problem areas. In this section, you'll focus on some of your challenges, but the point is not to beat yourself up over them. Instead, honestly acknowledging those faults is an important step toward recognizing how your old story has you trapped and how to break free from it.

So be candid with yourself here and also compassionate.

## RELATIONAL COSTS

Here are ways you may have hurt yourself and others in the past.

| | |
|---|---|
| 8 | The Eight's tendency to bulldoze people, look down on others' weaknesses, and not admit when they are in the wrong can push others away. |
| 9 | The Nine's chronic avoidance of conflict can be frustrating for loved ones, especially when it creates even more problems down the road. |
| 1 | The One's constant quest for perfection can make other people feel they don't measure up. |

| 2 | The Two's tendency to manipulate others to get love can wind up driving away the very people they want to love them. |
|---|---|
| 3 | The Three's focus on achievement can make other people feel they are just props whose job is to make the Three look successful. |
| 4 | The Four's emotional intensity and moodiness can be challenging, especially if the Four is sometimes needy and at other times pushes loved ones away. |
| 5 | The Five's emotional detachment can feel cold and alienating to loved ones, who feel shut out from their mental fortress. |
| 6 | The Six's regular state of anxiety and inability to make decisions can be frustrating to others, who get tired of reassuring the Six. |
| 7 | The Seven's need to avoid negativity means they might emotionally (or actually) abandon loved ones just when they need support. |

Has anyone ever accused you of behaving in the way your type is described here? If so, when and why?

What has your commitment to believing and living your old story cost other people? How has it hurt the people your care about?

What repetitive patterns are you sick and tired of in your relationships with the people closest to you?

What are the "unspoken rules" about how other people expect you to behave in keeping with your old story?

# BODILY COSTS

From the following list, circle any health issues you have experienced.

Chronic headaches or migraines

Insomnia/sleeplessness

Overeating

Heartburn

Stomachaches

Substance abuse

Rapid breathing/hyperventilating

Panic attacks

Depression

Anxiety

Autoimmune disorders

High blood pressure

Diabetes or high blood sugar

Racing heart

Light-headedness or fainting

Low sex drive

Muscle spasms or pain

If you have regularly experienced two or more health issues on this list, that may be a sign that you are under stress, since all of these issues can be stress-related.

Have you felt your body suffer because of the demands of the old story you've been telling yourself?

If so, how?

In the Enneagram, each triad has an associated "body center." These are:

| 8, 9, and 1 | The Gut Triad |
|---|---|
| 2, 3, and 4 | The Heart Triad |
| 5, 6, and 7 | The Head Triad |

Do you see any link between your type's "body center" and where you typically experience stress?

## OWN WHAT YOU WANT TO FORGET

Part of owning our shadow includes taking stock of the things we prefer not to think about. (It's tempting to skip this page because revisiting those things can be painful, but try to stick with it. An important step in changing your story is owning and integrating the things you would rather leave *out* of the story.)

**What feelings have you organized your life around avoiding? Helplessness? Fear? Inadequacy? Happiness? Love?**

What difficult or shameful events in your life have you not discussed with anyone, or just with one or two of the people closest to you?

When you remember those events that you prefer not to talk about, what is the main fear you have about confronting what happened?

Was any of this included in the "old story" you wrote in Step 2? If not, why do you think you omitted it?

What have you not taken responsibility for in your life?

What dreams have you given up on?

## WAKE UP TO YOUR OLD STORY

A major turning point in our journey to transformation is when we can step back and observe our default behaviors as they are happening in real time. Over the next pages, this log enables you to keep a record of times when you feel yourself slipping into your old story.

Try to keep this log over the course of several days, several times a day, even after you've moved forward to the next step. Keep coming back here and recording these events as they happen, whenever you feel yourself sliding back into your old story.

These will be little, daily things: a Three missed dinner with the family to put in extra hours at work, a Five fled from a conversation that threatened to get too personal, a Nine missed a deadline at work or school, or a One was overly critical of a family member. You may notice that the same things keep happening. Write them down even if—especially if!—they seem to be a pattern.

**What was the situation or trigger?**

**How did you react?**

How did that reaction reflect some of the weaknesses or problems of your Enneagram type?

How might you respond differently in the future?

**What was the situation or trigger?**

**How did you react?**

· · · · · · · · · · · · · · · · · · · · · · · · · · · · · · · · · · · · · · · · · · ·

How did that reaction reflect some of the weaknesses or problems of your Enneagram type?

How might you respond differently in the future?

**What was the situation or trigger?**

**How did you react?**

How did that reaction reflect some of the weaknesses or problems of your Enneagram type?

How might you respond differently in the future?

**What was the situation or trigger?**

**How did you react?**

How did that reaction reflect some of the weaknesses or problems of your Enneagram type?

How might you respond differently in the future?

**What was the situation or trigger?**

**How did you react?**

How did that reaction reflect some of the weaknesses or problems of your Enneagram type?

How might you respond differently in the future?

. . . . . . . . . . . . . . . . . . . . . . . . . . . . . . . . . . . . . . . . . . . . . . . . . . . . .

**What was the situation or trigger?**

**How did you react?**

How did that reaction reflect some of the weaknesses or problems of your Enneagram type?

How might you respond differently in the future?

**What was the situation or trigger?**

**How did you react?**

How did that reaction reflect some of the weaknesses or problems of your
Enneagram type?

How might you respond differently in the future?

What was the situation or trigger?

How did you react?

How did that reaction reflect some of the weaknesses or problems of your Enneagram type?

How might you respond differently in the future?

**What was the situation or trigger?**

**How did you react?**

How did that reaction reflect some of the weaknesses or problems of your Enneagram type?

How might you respond differently in the future?

**What was the situation or trigger?**




**How did you react?**

How did that reaction reflect some of the weaknesses or problems of your Enneagram type?

How might you respond differently in the future?

**What was the situation or trigger?**

**How did you react?**

How did that reaction reflect some of the weaknesses or problems of your Enneagram type?

How might you respond differently in the future?

What was the situation or trigger?

How did you react?

How did that reaction reflect some of the weaknesses or problems of your Enneagram type?

How might you respond differently in the future?

**What was the situation or trigger?**

**How did you react?**

How did that reaction reflect some of the weaknesses or problems of your Enneagram type?

How might you respond differently in the future?

What was the situation or trigger?

How did you react?

How did that reaction reflect some of the weaknesses or problems of your Enneagram type?

How might you respond differently in the future?

**What was the situation or trigger?**

**How did you react?**

How did that reaction reflect some of the weaknesses or problems of your Enneagram type?

How might you respond differently in the future?

# PART 2

# Inventory
# Your Strengths

From the time we enter this world, we begin crafting a story that helps us survive and guarantees a way to get what we need. From infancy, we learn through trial and error to manipulate and master our circumstances, and we continue doing that through childhood.

Each type's story—their new story redeemed out of the old, the tale told without wasting anything in our lives—reflects a beautiful, unique facet of God's holy character.

*—The Story of You*

Each Enneagram type is a mix of shadow and strengths. Just as it's important to own your struggles, it's also vital to inventory your strengths. Notice in the following table that the shorthand name given to every Enneagram type is something positive and constructive. The world needs helpers and romantics, challengers and loyalists. The world needs all nine types, as I discuss in the epilogue of *The Story of You.*

In short, the world needs *you.*

## INVENTORY YOUR STRENGTHS

In this exercise we're going to remember some of the best choices we've made and the constructive ways we've used our strengths in the past. When we can recognize these, we can see ourselves more wholistically and understand that the foundations for a new story are already inside us.

| | | Own Your Strengths |
|---|---|---|
| 8 | The Challenger | Commanding, bold, intense, capable, and protective leader |
| 9 | The Peacemaker | Gentle, affable, accommodating, humble, and calming mediator |

|   |   | Own Your Strengths |
|---|---|---|
| 1 | The Improver | Responsible, principled, strong, hardworking, and organized idealist |
| 2 | The Helper | Thoughtful, generous, selfless, compassionate, and encouraging caregiver |
| 3 | The Performer | Charming, adaptable, goal-oriented, confident, and successful pacesetter |
| 4 | The Romantic | Creative, emotional, original, intuitive, and sensitive visionary |
| 5 | The Investigator | Logical, impartial, curious, independent, and calm thinker |
| 6 | The Loyalist | Committed, supportive, community-oriented, trustworthy, stable team player |
| 7 | The Enthusiast | Adventurous, fun-loving, exuberant, energetic, and delightful free spirit |

This log enables you to keep a record of times when you capitalized on some of the strengths of your Enneagram type, so you can see how they might be assets in your ongoing development. Here we're focusing on things that happened in the past.

On the next six pages, reflect on key events that happened to you in the past and how you were able to cope successfully with adversity or thrive.

## Three Positive Experiences from Childhood

1. What was happening when you were called upon to rise above the situation?

What did you do that was positive or useful in that situation?

How did that response relate to the strengths of your particular Enneagram type?

2. What was happening when you were called upon to rise above the situation?

What did you do that was positive or useful in that situation?

How did that response relate to the strengths of your particular Enneagram type?

3. What was happening when you were called upon to rise above the situation?

What did you do that was positive or useful in that situation?

How did that response relate to the strengths of your particular Enneagram type?

# Three Positive Experiences from Adulthood

1. What was happening when you were called upon to rise above the situation?


What did you do that was positive or useful in that situation?


How did that response relate to the strengths of your particular Enneagram type?

2. What was happening when you were called upon to rise above the situation?

What did you do that was positive or useful in that situation?

How did that response relate to the strengths of your particular Enneagram type?

3. What was happening when you were called upon to rise above the situation?

What did you do that was positive or useful in that situation?

How did that response relate to the strengths of your particular Enneagram type?

## REMEMBER THE GIFTS OF YOUR OLD STORY

As you move from your old story and into a new one, it can be helpful to honor the things about your old story that helped you or were positive. We don't have to leave everything behind; we just need to sort through our experiences and narratives and decide which ones are worth keeping.

Here's an example. In the book *Re-Authoring the World*, Chené Swart tells about her own transformation out of her old story, which she called "Silent Servant." She was once a woman who was valued only for the way she quietly met other people's needs, asking nothing for herself. When that story began to take a terrible toll on her in adulthood, Swart knew she had to find her voice and change her life.

But rather than curse her old story, she decided to create a small ceremony in which she would thank Silent Servant for some of the gifts she had provided in Swart's life, such as teaching her to work hard, foster relationships with other people, and truly listen.

**What are some gifts the old story gave you, ones you want to carry forward? What have you liked about yourself?**

# Awaken

# PART 1

# Observing
# Your Patterns
# in Real Time

No one awakens in the morning, looks in the mirror, and says, "I think I will repeat my mistakes today," or "I expect that today I will do something really stupid, repetitive, regressive, and against my best interests." But, frequently, this replication of history is precisely what we do, because we are unaware of the silent presence of those programmed energies, the core ideas we have acquired, internalized, and surrendered to.

—James Hollis, *Finding Meaning in the Second Half of Life*

Mindfulness trains us to pay attention to what's happening in the present moment as we catch ourselves in the act of falling into our old story.

—*The Story of You*

In the See and Own steps, we focused primarily on the past—the stories and patterns that have dominated our understanding of ourselves since childhood. We named our old stories and identified which aspects were helpful and which were not.

Now with the Awaken step, we turn our attention to the present moment, to our lives right now. As you Awaken and become more mindful, you can begin to free yourself from the grip of your old story.

## CATCH YOURSELF IN THE ACT

Awakening happens with tiny acts, baby steps. On the next few pages, keep a record of the times you "catch yourself in the act" of following your old script.

To do this, it may be helpful to imagine yourself as an outside observer, standing apart from yourself and taking notes on what you do, when, and why. Try not to be judgmental or down on yourself about it—every time you catch yourself in the act, it's a learning experience and a stepping-stone to lasting change.

Here's a starter list of some of the behaviors and thoughts you may notice in yourself, depending on your Enneagram type. This is by no means exhaustive, but it may point you in the right direction as you begin to notice your own specific acts and attitudes.

**Observing Your Patterns in Real Time**

• • •

| | | Possible Behaviors You May Observe |
|---|---|---|
| 8 | The Challenger | ✓ Picking fights or wanting to get even with people who have wronged you.<br><br>✓ Demanding obedience and loyalty from others.<br><br>✓ Not listening to other people's views or opinions.<br><br>✓ Refusing to compromise.<br><br>✓ Dismissing weakness in others and concealing your vulnerability.<br><br>✓ Getting angry, sometimes excessively so, when things don't go your way or you feel out of control. |
| 9 | The Peacemaker | ✓ Going along with others just to keep the peace, even if you disagree.<br><br>✓ Looking to stronger, more energetic people to provide direction and initiative for your life.<br><br>✓ Numbing out; daydreaming; ignoring the real world.<br><br>✓ Procrastinating and getting distracted from tasks.<br><br>✓ Believing your preferences and opinions don't matter.<br><br>✓ Neglecting self-care. |

| | | Possible Behaviors You May Observe |
|---|---|---|
| 1 | The Improver | ✓ Criticizing yourself for not doing enough, or for doing things wrong.<br><br>✓ Judging other people as inferior or lacking.<br><br>✓ Thinking there is only one "right" way to do something, and lecturing others about how to do it.<br><br>✓ Believing it's your job to fix other people or their surroundings.<br><br>✓ Feeling embarrassed or even ashamed about your mistakes.<br><br>✓ Being overly controlling of your environment. |
| 2 | The Helper | ✓ Overextending yourself in helping others, even if they didn't ask for assistance.<br><br>✓ Feeling that your self-worth is tied up in whether other people like you.<br><br>✓ Creating dependencies in which other people have to rely on you regularly.<br><br>✓ Not asking for help when you need it yourself.<br><br>✓ Feeling entitled to other people's love because you showed them love first.<br><br>✓ Playing the martyr. |

**Observing Your Patterns in Real Time**

• • •

| | | Possible Behaviors You May Observe |
|---|---|---|
| **3** | The Performer | ✓ Going to great lengths to only let other people see the most successful or flattering version of yourself.<br><br>✓ Working too many hours, often at the expense of your relationships or your health.<br><br>✓ Chasing after status symbols, awards, or prestige.<br><br>✓ Changing your persona or image to impress whoever you're with at the moment.<br><br>✓ Taking shortcuts or embellishing the truth so you appear at the top of your game.<br><br>✓ Not acknowledging your own feelings. |
| **4** | The Romantic | ✓ Engaging in "push-pull" relationships, where you're overly needy and romanticizing someone one minute and pushing them away the next.<br><br>✓ Taking rejection or disappointment personally and intensely.<br><br>✓ Nursing old wounds from the past; or, at the other extreme, idealizing the past.<br><br>✓ Envying others.<br><br>✓ Overidentifying with your emotion of the moment.<br><br>✓ Fantasizing about the ideal past or future while thinking about what's missing in the present.<br><br>✓ Needing to stand apart as unique and special. |

| | | Possible Behaviors You May Observe |
|---|---|---|
| 5 | The Investigator | ✓ Withdrawing emotionally (and sometimes physically) from other people; being aloof or remote.<br>✓ Over-researching a decision, or staying in constant "research gathering" mode.<br>✓ Conflating your identity with your level of expertise.<br>✓ Hoarding your energy and seeing other people as draining.<br>✓ Disappearing into your mind, being removed from your body.<br>✓ Withholding information about yourself. |
| 6 | The Loyalist | ✓ Depending too much on the counsel of others.<br>✓ Anxiously imagining worst-case scenarios.<br>✓ Fearing that you're vulnerable without community support.<br>✓ Feeling suspicious of other people's motives.<br>✓ Mistrusting loved ones.<br>✓ Exaggerating what could go wrong.<br>✓ Leaning too heavily on a belief system or authority figure to tell you what to do. |

| | | Possible Behaviors You May Observe |
|---|---|---|
| **7** | The Enthusiast | ✓ Avoiding pain. |
| | | ✓ Needing constant entertainment or distraction. |
| | | ✓ Breaking prior commitments if something better comes along. |
| | | ✓ Immediately reframing anything negative into a positive. |
| | | ✓ Feeling trapped by routine or "ordinary" life. |
| | | ✓ Not finishing one task before jumping ahead to the next. |
| | | ✓ Having too many things going on at once. |

## MINDFULLY RESPONDING VS. MINDLESSLY REACTING

On these next pages, keep a close record of the small ways you can observe yourself thinking, feeling, and acting out your old story. Be sure to be compassionate toward yourself, no matter what is coming up for you.

Our goal is to move from *reacting* to *responding*. Reacting is what happens when we're on autopilot. We act blindly, sometimes destructively, without pausing to interrupt the circuit of our old story. When an Eight reacts to a stressful situation, it could be by exploding or blaming others; when a Three reacts, it could mean amplifying a story so they come out looking like a hero. Whatever your Enneagram type, you're probably familiar with what reacting can look like for you.

*Responding* is different. Responding is when you are able to hit the pause button and observe what you are feeling, thinking, and doing in the present moment. It's important to extend some compassion here. When you feel yourself caught in the grip of your old story, you might stand back and say, "Well, I'm certainly free to continue this way, but wouldn't it end better if I took my foot off the gas pedal and tried something else?"

On these next pages, keep a situation log of the things that happen to you and how you react or respond. These can be small things, such as how you feel when you have a conflict with a family member or how you handle a deadline or assignment at work.

**Observe the situation: What's happening right now?**

**What I'm thinking:**

**What I'm feeling:**

What I'm doing:

Am I responding or reacting?

Observe the situation: What's happening right now?

What I'm thinking:

. . . . . . . . . . . . . . . . . . . . . . . . . . . . . . . . . . . . . . . . . . . . . .

**What I'm feeling:**

**What I'm doing:**

. . . . . . . . . . . . . . . . . . . . . . . . . . . . . . . . . . . . . . . . . . . . . .

**Observing Your Patterns in Real Time**

• • •

Am I responding or reacting?

Observe the situation: What's happening right now?

What I'm thinking:

. . . . . . . . . . . . . . . . . . . . . . . . . . . . . . . . . . . . . . . . . . . . . . . . . . .

**What I'm feeling:**

**What I'm doing:**

. . . . . . . . . . . . . . . . . . . . . . . . . . . . . . . . . . . . . . . . . . . . . . . . . . .

Am I responding or reacting?

Observe the situation: What's happening right now?

What I'm thinking:

**What I'm feeling:**

**What I'm doing:**

**Observing Your Patterns in Real Time**

• • •

Am I responding or reacting?

**Observe the situation: What's happening right now?**

**What I'm thinking:**

**What I'm feeling:**

**What I'm doing:**

Am I responding or reacting?

Observe the situation: What's happening right now?

What I'm thinking:

**What I'm feeling:**

**What I'm doing:**

Am I responding or reacting?

Observe the situation: What's happening right now?

What I'm thinking:

What I'm feeling:

What I'm doing:

Am I responding or reacting?

Observe the situation: What's happening right now?

What I'm thinking:

**What I'm feeling:**

**What I'm doing:**

Am I responding or reacting?

Observe the situation: What's happening right now?

What I'm thinking:

**What I'm feeling:**

**What I'm doing:**

Am I responding or reacting?

# PART 2

# Agere Contra for Each Type

Here you learn the power of doing the opposite of what you would normally do, responding to difficult situations (and people) in new and creative ways. The goal is to challenge your old beliefs and narratives to help you get unstuck.

    *Agere contra* rests on the idea that we can . . . name whatever it is that owns us and is driving our behavior—our old story. Then we can actively choose to do something else instead. When it comes to the Enneagram, this means taking steps to reject your type's Passion and cultivate its Virtue.

—*The Story of You*

As we've seen, in the "Awaken" step we develop increased awareness and learn how to resist the gravitational pull of our old, familiar story. One way of thinking about that old story is that it is tied to our Enneagram Passion.

For the new story, we want to be moving toward our type's Virtue. We move from our Passion to our Virtue by doing the opposite of what our old story tells us to do, which is called *agere contra.*

## UNDERSTAND YOUR PASSION AND YOUR VIRTUE

As a reminder, here are the Passions and Virtues of each of the nine Enneagram types.

|  | Passion | Virtue |
|---|---|---|
| The Challenger: Eight | Lust | Innocence |
| The Peacemaker: Nine | Sloth | Right Action |
| The Improver: One | Anger | Serenity |
| The Helper: Two | Pride | Humility |

*Agere Contra* **for Each Type**

• • •

| | Passion | Virtue |
|---|---|---|
| **The Performer: Three** | Deceit | Authenticity |
| **The Romantic: Four** | Envy | Equanimity |
| **The Investigator: Five** | Avarice | Nonattachment |
| **The Loyalist: Six** | Fear | Courage |
| **The Enthusiast: Seven** | Gluttony | Sobriety |

Remember two important things about your Passion:

1. Your Passion is the root cause of your pain.
2. You will be ruled by your Passion until you can observe its hold on you and begin to disengage from it.

## PLAYING AGAINST TYPE

Sometimes we only become aware of the roles we are playing when we begin to behave differently than we have in the past, "playing against type." This is an example of *agere contra*: doing something different than our regular, default mode of behaving.

You likely have some experience already with *agere contra*. I want you to remember some times in your past when you *didn't* follow the dictates of your old story—the Nine suddenly took charge, the Seven turned introspective or chose to live in the present moment, or the One laughed off a mistake.

For the following questions, think about situations when you practiced *agere contra*, even if you didn't have a name for what you were doing.

## In Childhood

When you were a child, when did you push back against the role your old story demanded that you play? What was the situation?

Did other people notice when you began pushing against the boundaries of your old story? If so, how did they react?

How did the act of resisting your old story make you feel?

What stopped you from making that resistance a way of life?

## In Adolescence

· · · · · · ·

When you were a teenager, when did you push back against the role your old story demanded that you play? What was the situation?

Did other people notice when you began pushing against the boundaries of your old story? If so, how did they react?

How did the act of resisting your old story make you feel?

What stopped you from making that resistance a way of life?

## In Adulthood

Recently, as an adult, when did you push back against the role your old story demanded that you play? What was the situation?

Did other people notice when you began pushing against the boundaries of your old story? If so, how did they react?

How did the act of resisting your old story make you feel?

What stopped you from making that resistance a way of life?

# REACH FOR YOUR TYPE'S VIRTUE

Look over your written responses above. Pay particular attention in your answers to any positive things you felt after each decision *not* to behave according to your old story's dictates. Did you feel empowered? At peace? More true to yourself? More alive?

In the following table, explore what your type's Virtue can offer you as you begin to craft a new story, away from the grip of your Passion.

| | | |
|---|---|---|
| **8** | Innocence | When Eights recapture their Innocence, they can reveal—and delight in—the vulnerability they've taught themselves to bury deep down. |
| **9** | Right Action | Nines who embrace Right Action understand their own importance, accept conflict as part of life, and invest in their own development. |
| **1** | Serenity | Ones cultivate Serenity by accepting things as they are, not as they would have them. They transcend the trap of their Passion by realizing they're not responsible for improving everything around them. |
| **2** | Humility | Twos who practice Humility realize that they have needs too and that they don't have all of the time, treasure, and talent to help everyone. |

| 3 | Authenticity | Threes discover Authenticity when they understand they are valuable simply for who they are, not for what they achieve. They no longer feel the need to adjust their persona to suit an audience or be seen as more successful than they are. |
|---|---|---|
| 4 | Equanimity | Fours in Equanimity understand they are not being singled out for suffering and that they don't need to compare themselves to others. They are no longer driven by envy and experience a composed, emotionally balanced soul. |
| 5 | Nonattachment | Fives let go of their need to be entirely self-sufficient and seek out a full range of emotions. They become more present to other people and give more freely of themselves without hoarding their energy and time. |
| 6 | Courage | Sixes who practice Courage discover their own inner strength without needing to be validated by an external authority. They are not ruled by their fears, but rise above anxiety with a steadfast faith in the future. |
| 7 | Sobriety | Sevens who welcome Sobriety are able to slow down and recognize that what they already have is enough. They enjoy turning inward instead of requiring constant stimulation and excitement from outside themselves. |

*Agere Contra* **for Each Type**

• • •

What are a few small, specific things you can start doing today to move closer to your type's Virtue?

# Rewrite

# PART 1

# Naming and Imagining Your New Story

Waking up from our scripted trance, we realize we no longer have to sleepwalk as a character trapped in a destructive story. We wake up and consider new and different possibilities. We create a crossroads and turn a new direction. We claim authorship of our story rather than mere participation.

*—The Story of You*

When we cultivate awareness of our type tendencies, we learn to refrain from playing the same role in our old story, to create space so we can respond instead of react, and to reframe our perspective into a better story.

*—The Story of You*

Writing a new story is exciting and also a bit intimidating. It may feel like you are stepping off the ledge into unknown territory, but that's okay! It's also fine if this new story, singular, is really going to be new stories, plural. What you write here doesn't need to be fixed in stone. You will be adjusting and reimagining it as you grow and as your circumstances change. (For more on that, you can reread the epilogue, "Revise with Compassion," to *The Story of You*.)

Stepping into a new story is easier when you have a road map and a clear sense of where you want to go. Most meaningful journeys have a destination in mind. In this step, we'll give a title to your new story and also flesh out some details of what you want it to look like.

## TAKE A MINDFUL MOMENT

· · · · · · · · · · · · · · · · · · · · · · · · · · · · · · · · · · · · ·

Before you begin rewriting your story, I'd like you to pause and understand something important. *You are not rewriting your story alone.* There are grace and power in the universe to help you.

If you feel comfortable saying a prayer, please say this one aloud to state your commitment and seek divine help:

God, please help me craft my new story. Show me ways to break the old patterns that have held me back. Teach me to dream big while paying attention to the small steps and habits that lead to lasting change. Inspire me with a spark of your creativity and give me grace for the road ahead.

If you *aren't* comfortable praying to God, feel free to rewrite those words in a way that feels right to you, perhaps by focusing on your own initiative and role as a change agent ("May I find ways to break the old patterns").

**Are you generally more skillful at the "dreaming big" part of the equation for change, or the "small steps and habits" part?**

**Where might you need the most help?**

In what ways could you invite divine power into your life for regular, mindful help in rewriting your story?

## RENAME YOUR STORY

Look back to the first step at the beginning of the workbook (see "Your Enneagram Type's Origin Story"). Take a moment to reread what you wrote there about your old story and its impact on your life.

**The name of your old story was:**

In rewriting your story, a title is key. Often, as you name your new story, your Enneagram's Virtue can be a constructive guide, a reminder of what you're aiming for.

Here are a few possible examples from each type. These are not intended to limit you; they're only here as prompts. Feel free to adapt these to your own life or create something different, totally your own. They can be playful or serious.

| 8 | Innocence | "The Power of Vulnerability"<br>"The Innocence Project"<br>"Protector of the Weak"<br>"Leading without Controlling" |
|---|---|---|
| 9 | Right Action | "Just Do the Next Right Thing"<br>"Standing My Ground"<br>"Seeing and Being Seen"<br>"I'm Showing Up Today!" |
| 1 | Serenity | "Progress, Not Perfection"<br>"No More Mr./Ms. Fix-It"<br>"Good Enough"<br>"This Court Is Adjourned" |
| 2 | Humility | "Just Say No"<br>"Happiness from Within"<br>"Stop Keeping Score"<br>"Needy, Not Just Needed" |

| | | |
|---|---|---|
| **3** | Authenticity | "I'm More Than What I Do"<br>"The Best Life Is Not Instagrammable"<br>"Making Space for Feelings"<br>"It's Not a Competition" |
| **4** | Equanimity | "The Beauty Lover"<br>"I Am Not My Feelings"<br>"Everything I Need Is Already Here"<br>"Belonging to Myself" |
| **5** | Nonattachment | "Open Fortress"<br>"I'm Here for You"<br>"The Grinch's Small Heart Grew Three Sizes That Day"<br>"Transformation Beyond Information" |
| **6** | Courage | "I Am the Only Committee I Need"<br>"Braveheart"<br>"Perfect Love Casts Out Fear"<br>"I Pledge Allegiance" |
| **7** | Sobriety | "More Is Not Always Better"<br>"Staying the Course"<br>"Pain Is the Path to Growth"<br>"Satisfied" |

Some possible titles for your new story:

Final title of your new story:

# IMAGINE YOUR NEW STORY

Now that you have a working title for your new story, take a little time to dream aloud. On these next pages, respond to the prompts about what you want, and what you don't want, in your new story.

## Acknowledge the Negative

What patterns are you sick and tired of that you do *not* want to be part of your new story?

Whom do you need to forgive from your old story to move forward with the new?

What excuses do you make for *not* crafting a new story? (e.g., "I'm too old to make a difference;" "I can't repair all the mistakes I've made.")

How can you rewrite those excuses? (e.g., "I'm old enough that I owe it to myself and those I love to rewrite my story going forward;" "I've made mistakes that taught me great lessons and made me wiser, which will help me craft a better story.")

# Embrace the Future

· · · · · · · · · ·

In a perfect world, what do you want to be doing in three to five years?

What values or beliefs do you want to make space for in your new story?

What people or relationships do you want to make space for in your new story?

What can you do right now to help make your new story a reality?

# PART 2

# Writing and Sharing Your New Story

You are the author of your own life story. You have the leading role and get to determine how you interact with your supporting cast and other characters. Without realizing it, you may have allowed the events in your life to write your story for you rather than taking deliberate action to write it in your own voice. What will it take to love your life story to create the happy endings you desire?

—Susan C. Young

Your new story is already alive and well in you; we just need to practice letting it emerge.

—*The Story of You*

All of the previous steps have been building to this point: knowing that we have the power to rewrite our stories. Now we will actually write or dictate a new story for ourselves, embracing our power to *respond* and not just *react.*

You may feel intimidated by the act of writing and toy with the idea of skipping this step. Please don't. There is something powerful about declaring your new story on paper. It means you're ready to claim authorship of your future.

## PUT IT ON PAPER

Just as you did in the "See" step when you wrote your old story, set a timer for twenty to thirty minutes. Let yourself visualize a new story without judgment or limitations. This is your time to SOAR, so gently quiet any voices in your head that may be saying, "That'll never happen."

It's possible that when you wrote your old story in the "See" step, you pegged yourself as the villain, the victim, or just a passive observer. Here, though, I want you to rewrite your story with yourself as the hero. This is a simple but powerful shift: How would your life change if you embraced the role of the hero?

As you write, you may wish to go back through your workbook and revisit what you wrote in previous steps about how the old story of your Enneagram type sometimes got in the way of your relationships, work, and happiness. Writing your new story gives you the chance to imagine a new life of mindfully responding to life rather than simply reacting.

What do you want to change? *Write it down.* (If you're terrified of the blank page, you can "write" by speaking your new story out loud into a dictation app and then using the resulting text as a starting point for what you write down here.)

**Name of new story:**

**Story:**

# SHARE YOUR NEW STORY

Here's a final exercise for your Rewrite step. Just as writing your story on paper can establish your concrete intentions for change, so too can sharing your new story with a trusted loved one (or group). There is deep vulnerability when you reveal your deepest hopes to another person, and powerful accountability when you lay out your plans for lasting transformation.

Ideally you will be reading your new story aloud to this person. If that's too hard or raw for you, just show them this journal and then talk about it. You may not need any prompts at all for that conversation, but if you do, here are some ideas to guide you.

**Name of my old story:**

**Name of my new story:**

The messages my old story told me:

My Enneagram type's Passion and Virtue:

The practical steps I'm taking to practice *agere contra* and move toward my type's Virtue:

The hopes I have for my life in three to five years:

**What will change now that I am the hero of my own story:**

**What you can do to help me inhabit my new story faithfully:**

Be sure to express your gratitude that this loved one is in your life and can be trusted with your deepest, most authentic self.

# CELEBRATE!

While we know that the path to transformation is the work of a lifetime, we can also celebrate the self-awareness we've achieved and the commitment we've made to crafting a different future.

It's time to recognize all the hard inner work you've been doing. You've faced some difficult truths about yourself and come out stronger! Celebrate the new story of you.